REAL ESTATE INVESTING GUIDE FOR BEGINNERS

Andy E. Long

Copyright © 2024 by Andy E. Long
All rights reserved.

No part of this publication may be reproduced, distributed, or transmitted in any form or by any means, including photocopying, recording, or other electronic or mechanical methods, without the prior written permission of the publisher, except in the case of brief quotations embodied in critical reviews and certain other noncommercial uses permitted by copyright law.

Legal Disclaimer

The information provided in this book is intended for educational purposes only. The content is not to be construed as legal, financial, or investment advice. While every effort has been made to ensure the accuracy and reliability of the information contained herein, the author and publisher make no representations or warranties regarding the completeness, accuracy, or timeliness of the content.

Real estate investing involves risk, and the reader should conduct their own due diligence and seek professional advice before making any investment decisions. The author and publisher shall not be held liable for any losses, damages, or adverse consequences arising from the use or application of any information presented in this book.

By reading this book, you acknowledge and agree that the author and publisher are not responsible for any personal decisions, financial actions, or outcomes that may result from following the information provided.

Dedication

To those who dare to take the first step,
To the aspiring investors with big dreams and bold ambitions,
And to everyone who believes that building wealth through real estate is not just for the few,
but for anyone willing to learn, grow, and take action.

This book is for you.

TABLE OF CONTENT

INTRODUCTION 10
    WHY REAL ESTATE IS A SMART INVESTMENT 14
    WHAT YOU CAN EXPECT FROM THIS GUIDE 17

CHAPTER 1: UNDERSTANDING REAL ESTATE INVESTING 21
    THE BASICS OF PROPERTY INVESTMENT 25
    KEY TERMS EVERY BEGINNER SHOULD KNOW 27
    TYPES OF REAL ESTATE INVESTMENTS 30

CHAPTER 2: ASSESSING YOUR FINANCES 35
    UNDERSTANDING YOUR BUDGET AND FINANCIAL GOALS 40
    HOW TO SECURE FINANCING FOR YOUR FIRST INVESTMENT 42
    THE IMPORTANCE OF CREDIT SCORES IN REAL ESTATE 45

CHAPTER 3: FINDING THE RIGHT PROPERTY 49
    HOW TO CHOOSE A PROFITABLE MARKET .. 55

EVALUATING PROPERTY TYPES: RESIDENTIAL, COMMERCIAL, AND MORE... 57
WHAT MAKES A GOOD INVESTMENT PROPERTY 60

CHAPTER 4: ANALYZING POTENTIAL RETURNS 64

THE NUMBERS YOU NEED TO KNOW 68
HOW TO CALCULATE CASH FLOW AND ROI 71
USING COMPARATIVE MARKET ANALYSIS (CMA) 73

CHAPTER 5: FINANCING YOUR INVESTMENT 77

TRADITIONAL FINANCING VS. ALTERNATIVE METHODS 82
UNDERSTANDING MORTGAGES, LOANS, AND DOWN PAYMENTS 85
CREATIVE FINANCING OPTIONS FOR BEGINNERS 88

CHAPTER 6: MANAGING YOUR PROPERTY 91

THE BASICS OF PROPERTY MANAGEMENT . 96
HOW TO FIND AND SCREEN TENANTS 98
MAINTENANCE, REPAIRS, AND LEGAL RESPONSIBILITIES 100

CHAPTER 7: MINIMIZING RISK AND MAXIMIZING PROFIT 104

UNDERSTANDING MARKET CYCLES AND TRENDS 109
HOW TO MITIGATE RISKS IN PROPERTY INVESTMENT 111
STRATEGIES FOR INCREASING PROPERTY VALUE 114

CHAPTER 8: SCALING YOUR REAL ESTATE PORTFOLIO 118

WHEN AND HOW TO EXPAND YOUR INVESTMENTS 122
USING LEVERAGE TO GROW YOUR PORTFOLIO 125
DIVERSIFYING YOUR REAL ESTATE HOLDINGS 127

CHAPTER 9: TAX IMPLICATIONS AND BENEFITS 130

HOW REAL ESTATE INVESTMENT AFFECTS YOUR TAXES 134
DEDUCTIONS AND CREDITS EVERY INVESTOR SHOULD KNOW 136
LONG-TERM TAX STRATEGIES FOR PROPERTY INVESTORS 139

CHAPTER 10: COMMON PITFALLS TO AVOID **142**

MISTAKES FIRST-TIME INVESTORS MAKE 147

HOW TO AVOID OVERPAYING FOR PROPERTY 149

NAVIGATING LEGAL AND REGULATORY CHALLENGES 151

CONCLUSION: YOUR PATH TO BUILDING WEALTH **154**

HOW TO STAY FOCUSED AND CONTINUE GROWING 158

SETTING LONG-TERM INVESTMENT GOALS 160

THE POWER OF PATIENCE IN REAL ESTATE 162

Introduction

"Real estate is not just about property; it's about creating wealth, generating cash flow, and building a legacy."

The world of real estate investing has long been viewed as a path to financial freedom, but for many beginners, it can feel like an intimidating and complex landscape. For the novice investor, the abundance of terminology, market dynamics, and seemingly endless investment options can quickly become overwhelming. However, there's good news: You don't need a background in finance or decades of experience to begin building wealth through real estate. In fact, all it takes is a shift in mindset and a strategic approach to get started.

In the next few pages, you'll discover that real estate investing isn't some elusive secret known only to a select few. It's a powerful tool that anyone can use—regardless of age, background, or current financial situation. Whether you're looking to create passive income, build long-term wealth, or simply make your money work for you, real estate offers a range of opportunities to meet your goals. The key lies in understanding how to navigate the process and avoid the common pitfalls that many first-time investors fall into.

What makes real estate so appealing, especially in today's market, is its stability. Unlike the stock market, which can fluctuate wildly from one day to the next, real estate tends to offer more consistent returns over time. With the right strategies, you can enjoy not only the benefits of property appreciation but also the recurring cash flow from rental income. Even in challenging economic times, real estate has proven to be a reliable investment vehicle, often outperforming other forms of investment.

But what's truly exciting is the way technology has transformed the real estate investing landscape. Gone are the days when you had to be physically present to monitor markets, analyze properties, or even secure financing. Today, digital platforms, online tools, and artificial intelligence are giving investors unprecedented access to market data, property listings, and financing options. The ability to research, evaluate, and manage investments has never been easier or more accessible to the everyday investor.

Yet, despite the many advancements, one thing remains crucial: financial literacy. Understanding the financial aspects of real estate is not only important for making smart investment choices but also for building long-term wealth. Knowing how to calculate potential returns, assess risks, and structure deals is what separates successful investors from those who get burned. This is where many beginners falter. It's not enough to jump into the market hoping for success— knowledge and strategy are your best allies.

As you embark on this journey, keep in mind that real estate is not a get-rich-quick venture. It's a long-term play that requires patience, careful planning, and a willingness to learn. But with persistence, the rewards are substantial. Whether you're eyeing a single-family rental, a commercial property, or a multi-unit apartment building, the principles you'll learn in this book will help you build a foundation for wealth that can last for generations.

So, take a deep breath, and know that the path ahead is one of growth, learning, and opportunity. By the end of this guide, you'll have the knowledge, tools, and strategies needed to make informed decisions and confidently step into the world of real estate investing. Let's get started.

Why Real Estate is a Smart Investment

When you think of building wealth, real estate often stands out as a cornerstone. It's been a reliable investment for centuries, and its ability to generate consistent returns is why so many consider it a smart choice. Unlike stocks or bonds, the value of real estate typically appreciates over time, providing investors with both short-term cash flow and long-term capital gains.

Real estate is unique because it offers multiple streams of income. First, there's the potential for monthly rental income, which can provide a steady cash flow. This makes it an ideal choice for those looking to create passive income without relying entirely on their salary. If managed well, rental properties can generate income for decades, long after the initial purchase price has been covered.

Then, there's the opportunity for capital appreciation. As neighborhoods grow and develop, property values tend to increase. This means that the property you invest in today could be worth much more in a few years. Unlike stocks, which can experience volatility from one day to the next, real estate typically sees more stable, predictable growth, making it a safer bet in the long term.

Moreover, real estate provides leverage. This means you can control a property worth much more than your initial investment by using financing options like mortgages. With just a down payment, you can acquire an asset that has the potential to increase in value, all while generating rental income. This ability to borrow money and still earn a return on the full value of the property is what makes real estate a truly unique and powerful investment vehicle.

One of the most attractive aspects of real estate is that it's a tangible asset. Unlike digital stocks or bonds, you can physically see and touch your investment. You have direct control over how the property is managed, maintained, and improved. The ability to renovate or upgrade a property allows you to directly influence its value and, in turn, the return on your investment. Real estate also serves as a hedge against inflation—property values and rents generally rise with inflation, helping to protect the investor's wealth.

Finally, real estate offers significant tax benefits. Investors can take advantage of deductions for mortgage interest, property taxes, insurance, and other expenses. Depreciation also allows investors to reduce taxable income, even though the property may be increasing in value. These benefits can significantly enhance the returns on your investment, making real estate even more attractive.

In short, real estate remains one of the most reliable, flexible, and profitable ways to grow wealth over time. Whether you're looking for a stable income source, long-term appreciation, or both, real estate checks all the boxes.

What You Can Expect from This Guide

This guide is designed to take you through the journey of real estate investing step-by-step. If you're new to the world of property investment, don't worry—this book is written with you in mind. We're going to break down the complex concepts, strategies, and methods into digestible pieces, so you can understand the process and begin investing with confidence.

We'll start with the very basics. You'll learn what real estate investing is, why it's a good choice for creating wealth, and the key terms that every beginner needs to know. By the end of this guide, you'll be able to talk the talk, understanding terms like ROI, cap rates, and cash flow.

Next, we'll dive into how to assess your financial situation and determine how much you can afford to invest. One of the most critical mistakes new investors make is jumping into a deal without fully understanding their financial position. This guide will teach you how to analyze your current assets, debts, and goals, so you can make informed, realistic decisions.

The following chapters will focus on finding the right property for your goals. Real estate isn't a one-size-fits-all investment, and choosing the wrong property can cost you time and money. You'll learn how to research neighborhoods, assess potential rental income, and evaluate whether a property fits your financial objectives.

We'll also cover how to finance your investments—because let's face it, unless you have a substantial amount of cash on hand, you'll likely need financing to get started. Whether it's a traditional mortgage, private lender, or creative financing option, you'll get a clear understanding of your options and how to secure the funding you need to make your first purchase.

As you gain knowledge, we'll guide you through the steps of managing your property efficiently, including dealing with tenants, handling maintenance, and maximizing your profits. From there, you'll learn how to scale your real estate portfolio, growing your assets and wealth with each new property you acquire.

We'll also take a deep dive into tax benefits, risk management, and strategies for mitigating losses, ensuring that you're protected and maximizing your investment potential.

Ultimately, this guide is not just about helping you make your first purchase; it's about equipping you with the knowledge to thrive in real estate. It's about learning how to think like a successful investor, set long-term goals, and create a sustainable strategy for building wealth. By the time you've read through this guide, you'll have the tools you need to start your real estate journey and confidently take the first step toward securing your financial future.

So, buckle up. The world of real estate investing is waiting for you, and with this guide in hand, you're ready to take on the challenge.

Chapter 1: Understanding Real Estate Investing

"Real estate is the closest thing to a proverbial goldmine."

Real estate investing is often seen as the holy grail of wealth-building, but what does it actually mean to invest in property? Simply put, real estate investing is the act of purchasing, owning, managing, or selling properties for profit. Whether it's buying a single-family home to rent out or investing in a large commercial building, the fundamentals of real estate investing remain largely the same.

At its core, real estate investing involves leveraging the value of physical assets—properties—to generate income, create equity, and build long-term wealth. Unlike stocks, which fluctuate in value based on market trends, real estate tends to provide more stability, offering investors a tangible asset that can appreciate over time. While the stock market can be unpredictable and volatile, real estate often grows steadily, providing consistent returns through rental income and property value appreciation. It's a powerful wealth-building tool that allows investors to use leverage (borrowed money) to control properties worth far more than their initial investment.

There are several different ways to invest in real estate, and it's crucial to understand each one before diving in. One of the most common methods is purchasing rental properties. This could be anything from a small apartment to a large commercial property. The primary benefit of rental properties is cash flow—once the property is paid off, you can collect rent for years to come, creating a steady income stream. This is one of the most attractive features of real estate investment, as it allows investors to earn passive income while their property appreciates in value.

But rental properties are just one piece of the real estate puzzle. Other forms of real estate investment include flipping houses, investing in real estate investment trusts (REITs), and buying land for future development. House flipping involves purchasing undervalued properties, renovating them, and selling them at a profit. This strategy requires a keen eye for value, a solid understanding of the renovation process, and the ability to manage risks associated with property value fluctuations. REITs, on the other hand, allow investors to invest in real estate without physically owning property. By purchasing shares in a REIT, you can profit from the income generated by large-scale real estate portfolios, such as shopping malls, office buildings, and apartment complexes.

Understanding the terminology and key concepts of real estate is vital before making your first investment. Terms like cash flow, equity, appreciation, cap rate, and ROI (return on investment) will become central to your decision-making process. Real estate investors evaluate these metrics to assess the potential profitability of an investment property. Knowing how to calculate them, and understanding what they mean in real-world terms, will give you a solid foundation for making informed decisions.

While real estate investing offers significant opportunities for profit, it's not without its risks. Market fluctuations, changing interest rates, unexpected maintenance costs, and tenant issues can all affect the profitability of a property. But with the right knowledge, planning, and a strategic approach, these risks can be managed effectively.

As you begin to explore the world of real estate, it's essential to remember that investing in property is not a get-rich-quick endeavor. It requires patience, strategy, and a long-term vision. But for those willing to put in the work, the rewards are well worth the effort. The ability to generate passive income, build equity, and accumulate wealth over time makes real estate investing an appealing choice for anyone looking to take control of their financial future. Let's dive deeper into the different strategies and concepts that can help you succeed in this exciting field.

The Basics of Property Investment

Real estate investing involves the purchase, ownership, management, rental, or sale of properties for profit. At its most basic, real estate investing is about acquiring physical assets—properties—that can provide income or appreciate in value over time. The beauty of real estate is that it's not just a place to live; it's also a wealth-building tool. With the right strategy, property investments can deliver reliable returns, diversify your financial portfolio, and offer long-term financial security.

There are many ways to invest in real estate, but it always begins with acquiring an asset— whether it's a single-family home, a commercial building, or a plot of land. What distinguishes real estate from other investment opportunities, such as stocks or bonds, is that it's tangible. You can see and touch the property, and it has an inherent value beyond just its market price. Real estate investing can take different forms, but the most common methods involve either earning income from the property or waiting for the value of the property to increase, then selling for a profit.

Property investments are often considered safer than other forms of investment, especially stocks, because they tend to be less volatile. While the stock market can swing wildly from day to day, the value of real estate tends to appreciate more steadily over time. Though there are risks involved, real estate's ability to generate passive income and provide tangible value makes it a preferred choice for many long-term investors. As long as you do your due diligence, understand market trends, and properly manage the investment, real estate can be a consistent source of wealth.

Key Terms Every Beginner Should Know

Before you dive into real estate investing, it's crucial to understand some key terms and concepts that will be used throughout your journey. These terms are the foundation of making informed decisions about your investments and ensuring you're on the path to profitability.

- **Return on Investment (ROI):** ROI is a key metric for assessing the profitability of an investment. It measures the return generated by an investment as a percentage of the initial cost. For example, if you bought a property for $100,000 and made $10,000 in rental income or profit from selling it, your ROI would be 10%. The higher the ROI, the better the return on your investment.

- **Capitalization Rate (Cap Rate):** The cap rate is a ratio used to estimate the return on a real estate investment. It's calculated by dividing the annual net operating income (NOI) of a property by its current market value or purchase price. This helps investors evaluate the profitability of a property relative to its price. For example, if a property generates $20,000 in net operating income annually and is valued at $250,000, the cap rate is 8% ($20,000 ÷ $250,000). Cap rates can vary depending on the type of property and the location.

- **Equity:** Equity refers to the difference between the market value of a property and the amount owed on any mortgages or loans. For example, if a property is worth $300,000 and you still owe $150,000 on your mortgage, your equity in the property is $150,000. As you pay down the mortgage, your equity increases, which is a form of wealth-building over time.

- **Cash Flow:** Cash flow is the amount of money a property generates after all expenses have been paid. This includes mortgage payments, property taxes, insurance, maintenance costs, and management fees. Positive cash flow means that the property is generating more income than expenses, which is the goal for most investors. Negative cash flow, on the other hand, means that the property is costing you more than it's bringing in, which could lead to financial strain.

- **Appreciation:** Appreciation refers to the increase in the value of a property over time. While properties don't always appreciate in value, historically, real estate tends to appreciate in stable markets. Appreciation is a key factor in long-term wealth-building because it allows investors to sell their properties for a profit, sometimes years after purchase.

Understanding these terms is essential to evaluating potential investments and ensuring that you're making informed decisions. These metrics are what investors use to determine whether a property is worth purchasing and whether it will deliver the returns they expect.

Types of Real Estate Investments

When it comes to real estate, there are several types of investments to consider, each with its own set of benefits, risks, and financial goals. Understanding these different types will help you determine which one aligns best with your financial objectives and risk tolerance.

- Residential Properties: Residential real estate includes single-family homes, multi-family units (such as duplexes, triplexes, or apartment buildings), and vacation rentals. This is the most common form of real estate investment, especially for beginners. Residential properties offer the opportunity for rental income and long-term capital appreciation. Single-family homes tend to be easier to manage and finance, making them ideal for investors just starting out. Multi-family properties, on the other hand, offer higher income potential by generating rental income from multiple units.

- Commercial Real Estate: Commercial properties include office buildings, shopping centers, industrial parks, and hotels. Commercial real estate can offer higher returns than residential properties, but it also comes with increased risk and complexity. The income from commercial properties is generally more stable due to long-term leases with businesses rather than individual tenants. However, these properties tend to be more expensive and harder to finance, and the management can be more involved. Commercial real estate is typically more suitable for seasoned investors with larger capital reserves.

- **Real Estate Investment Trusts (REITs):** REITs are companies that own, operate, or finance income-producing real estate. They allow investors to pool their money to invest in large-scale commercial properties like office buildings, shopping malls, or hotels without actually owning the physical properties. REITs offer liquidity since they're publicly traded on stock exchanges, making them an attractive option for people who want to invest in real estate but don't have the capital or time to buy property directly. REITs pay dividends to investors based on the rental income generated by the properties they own, making them a solid option for those seeking passive income.

- **Land Investment:** Investing in raw land involves purchasing vacant land that has the potential for future development or appreciation. While land doesn't generate immediate income like rental properties, it can be a valuable long-term investment. Investors often look for properties in areas that are likely to see population growth, infrastructure development, or land-use changes. Land investment can be more speculative than other types of real estate, but it offers potential for high returns if done correctly.

- Fix-and-Flip Properties: This type of investment involves purchasing a distressed property at a lower price, renovating it, and then selling it for a profit. This can be a lucrative option for investors with a keen eye for property value and the ability to manage renovation projects. However, fix-and-flip investing carries higher risks since market conditions can affect the property's resale value, and renovation costs may exceed initial estimates.

Each type of real estate investment has its own set of advantages and challenges, but they all share the potential to generate income, build equity, and create long-term wealth. As you explore these options, it's essential to consider your goals, financial capacity, and risk tolerance to choose the right path for your investment strategy. Real estate offers something for everyone, from the beginner looking to buy a small rental property to the seasoned investor seeking larger commercial projects or REITs. Understanding your investment options is the first step to success in this dynamic and rewarding field.

Chapter 2: Assessing Your Finances

"An investment in knowledge pays the best interest." – Benjamin Franklin

Before diving headfirst into real estate, it's crucial to get a clear picture of your financial situation. Real estate is a significant financial commitment, and understanding your finances will help you make smarter, more strategic decisions as you embark on this journey. Your ability to invest successfully in property isn't just about finding the right deals; it's also about being prepared financially to handle the ups and downs of the market.

When assessing your finances, you need to take a step back and look at both your income and your expenses, your savings, and your debts. The goal here isn't just to see how much money you have in the bank today—it's about creating a roadmap for where you want to be in the future and how real estate fits into that vision.

First, start by determining your current financial standing. This means calculating your net worth, which is essentially the value of everything you own minus the debts you owe. If you're unsure of where you stand, this can be a great starting point. Make a list of all your assets—your home, savings, investments, and any property you own—and subtract any liabilities, such as student loans, credit card debt, and mortgages. Knowing your net worth is essential because it gives you a sense of your financial capacity to take on new investments.

Next, take a close look at your monthly income and expenses. This isn't just about what you earn, but also about how much you're spending. Are there areas where you can cut back to save more for your real estate investments? The goal is to create a budget that allows you to set aside enough capital for a down payment and emergency savings while still covering your current living expenses. Real estate investments often require significant upfront capital, so having a firm understanding of your monthly cash flow will help you determine how much you can afford to invest.

Your credit score is another critical factor to consider. Real estate investors often rely on loans to finance their purchases, and a good credit score can make a significant difference in securing favorable loan terms. If your credit score isn't where you want it to be, consider taking steps to improve it before applying for a mortgage. This could include paying down existing debt, avoiding late payments, and reducing your overall credit utilization.

Once you have a good handle on your personal finances, think about your long-term goals. How much are you hoping to earn from real estate? Are you planning to buy a rental property, flip houses, or invest in commercial real estate? The type of investment you choose will dictate how much capital you need to get started and how much risk you're willing to take on. Residential properties, for example, may require less initial capital, while commercial properties and large-scale developments may require significant financing.

Investing in real estate also comes with costs beyond just the purchase price. Consider the ongoing expenses, such as property taxes, insurance, maintenance, and management fees. Having a realistic understanding of the total cost of ownership will help you avoid surprises down the road.

Lastly, it's wise to have a cushion for unexpected expenses. Real estate investments can be unpredictable, and having a reserve fund will protect you in case of vacancies, property damage, or unforeseen market shifts. This financial cushion provides peace of mind and ensures that you can weather any storms that come your way.

Getting your finances in order before making a real estate investment isn't just a precaution—it's a crucial step in ensuring your long-term success. By taking the time to assess your financial health and plan accordingly, you'll be in a stronger position to make smart, confident investments that align with your goals. Remember, real estate is a marathon, not a sprint. Preparing financially gives you the foundation you need to succeed over time and helps you avoid the costly mistakes that come with jumping in too quickly without a clear plan. Now that you have a solid grasp on your financial standing, you're ready to explore how to make your first real estate investment a reality.

Understanding Your Budget and Financial Goals

Before you dive into the world of real estate investing, it's essential to understand your financial situation. Real estate is not a quick-flip market; it's a long-term commitment that requires careful planning and significant resources. Your ability to make smart, informed decisions largely depends on having a solid grasp of your finances, which starts with understanding your budget and setting clear investment goals.

The first step is calculating your current financial standing. Begin by taking an inventory of your assets and liabilities. Your assets include everything you own that holds value—your savings, investments, property, and even personal items like vehicles. Liabilities, on the other hand, are what you owe—credit card debt, loans, mortgages, or any other financial obligations. Subtract your liabilities from your assets to determine your net worth. This gives you a snapshot of your overall financial health.

Once you have a clear understanding of your net worth, it's time to evaluate your cash flow. This refers to how much money you have coming in and going out each month. Start by tracking your income (salaries, business revenue, side hustles) and compare it to your monthly expenses (housing, utilities, groceries, transportation). The goal is to identify any areas where you can cut back or reallocate funds toward your real estate investments. Creating a budget that accounts for both your immediate needs and long-term investment goals will help ensure that you're financially ready for the responsibility of owning property.

Setting realistic investment goals is a crucial part of the budgeting process. How much capital do you have available to invest, and how much more do you need to raise? Are you looking for a rental property that generates monthly cash flow, or are you more interested in flipping properties for a one-time profit? The size and scope of your investment goals will directly impact your required budget. Remember, starting small doesn't mean you can't scale up. Set short-term goals that align with your financial capacity while keeping long-term objectives in mind. For example, your first goal might be to save for a down payment on a rental property, with the idea that over time, you'll expand your portfolio.

How to Secure Financing for Your First Investment

One of the most intimidating aspects of real estate investing is securing financing, especially if you're new to the game. But understanding how to fund your real estate ventures is essential for building your portfolio and scaling your investments. There are several options available for financing a property, each with its own set of requirements and conditions.

The most common route for new real estate investors is a mortgage loan, particularly a conventional loan from a bank or credit union. To secure this type of financing, you'll typically need to put down a percentage of the property's purchase price, often 20% or more, though there are options for lower down payments. The loan will be repaid over a set period, typically 15 to 30 years, with fixed or variable interest rates. Your ability to secure a mortgage is largely based on your credit score, income, and overall financial health. Lenders will look at these factors to determine whether you are financially capable of repaying the loan.

In addition to traditional mortgages, you might consider other financing methods, such as private lenders or hard money loans. Private lenders are individuals or companies who lend money to real estate investors in exchange for a return on investment. These loans typically come with higher interest rates and shorter repayment terms but are easier to qualify for, especially if your credit isn't stellar. Hard money loans are another option, often used for short-term projects like house flipping. These loans are secured by the property itself, meaning the lender can seize the property if you fail to repay the loan.

Another alternative for securing financing is house hacking. This involves purchasing a multi-unit property, living in one unit, and renting out the others. This strategy allows you to use the rental income to cover your mortgage and property expenses, essentially living for free while building equity in the property.

Regardless of the financing option you choose, it's important to thoroughly research the terms and conditions, as well as compare interest rates and fees. Make sure that the monthly payments will be manageable given your cash flow. Don't forget to account for additional costs, such as property taxes, insurance, maintenance, and potential vacancies.

The Importance of Credit Scores in Real Estate

Your credit score plays a critical role in your ability to secure financing for real estate investments. Lenders use your credit score to assess your financial trustworthiness and determine the risk they're taking on by lending you money. A higher score typically means that you'll qualify for better loan terms, including lower interest rates, smaller down payments, and more favorable repayment schedules.

If your credit score is less than stellar, it doesn't mean real estate investing is off the table. However, it does mean that you might have to put in more effort to secure financing. For example, you may need a larger down payment or may be offered a higher interest rate to offset the risk. In some cases, it might be worthwhile to take a step back and work on improving your credit before pursuing your first property. Paying off outstanding debts, avoiding late payments, and reducing credit card balances can help improve your score over time.

For those new to credit, or those with poor scores, FHA loans (Federal Housing Administration loans) are a helpful option. These loans are designed to help individuals with lower credit scores or limited financial history purchase homes. The downside is that these loans are often only available for primary residences, meaning they wouldn't work for investment properties unless you plan to live in the property and rent out part of it.

You can also consider working with a co-signer or joint venture partner if your credit score isn't strong enough. A co-signer can help you secure a loan by agreeing to be responsible for the debt if you default. Joint ventures allow investors to pool resources and combine their creditworthiness to secure financing for a property purchase.

It's important to remember that your credit score isn't just a number; it's a reflection of your overall financial behavior. Keeping your credit in good standing is an ongoing process that will pay off in the long run, making it easier for you to access financing and negotiate favorable terms as you build your real estate portfolio. Start by understanding where your credit stands, and take steps to improve it if necessary—this will put you in a stronger position when you're ready to secure financing for your investment.

Real estate investing requires more than just capital—it requires careful financial planning, understanding of loan products, and a solid grasp of how credit affects your financing options. With the right approach, you can secure the funds needed for your first investment and set yourself up for success in the world of real estate. By budgeting effectively, setting realistic goals, and improving your credit score, you'll be well on your way to making smart and sustainable investments that align with your financial aspirations.

Chapter 3: Finding the Right Property

"Opportunities are usually disguised as hard work, so most people don't recognize them." – Ann Landers

The search for the perfect property is often the most exciting and overwhelming part of real estate investing. With so many options available, how do you know which property will be the right fit for your investment strategy? The answer lies in understanding your goals, researching the market, and narrowing down the possibilities to find the property that offers the best potential for long-term growth and profitability.

When you begin your search for a property, it's important to have a clear vision of what you're looking for. Are you seeking a fix-and-flip project that will provide quick returns, or are you looking for a buy-and-hold rental property that will generate passive income for years to come? The property you choose should align with your financial goals and your strategy for growth. Knowing your investment criteria ahead of time will help you avoid falling into the trap of buying properties that look appealing on the surface but may not fit your long-term objectives.

One of the first things to consider is the location of the property. Location is often said to be the most important factor in real estate because it determines everything from the property's value to its rental potential. A great location attracts tenants and future buyers, while a bad location can hinder your investment success. Look for areas that are experiencing growth in both property values and demand for rentals. Consider factors such as proximity to schools, public transport, major employers, and amenities like parks and shopping centers. These elements make a property more desirable and can increase its resale value down the line.

Once you've identified promising locations, it's time to dig into the specifics of the property. Whether you're buying a single-family home, a multi-family building, or a commercial property, each type comes with its own set of considerations. For residential properties, evaluate the neighborhood's vibe—are homes well-maintained, and is it a safe area? For multi-family buildings, assess the property's cash flow potential by looking at the number of units, current rental rates, and occupancy levels. A property with multiple units may provide a steady stream of income, but you'll need to calculate whether the rental income will cover all costs, including mortgage payments, property management fees, taxes, and maintenance.

For those considering commercial real estate, the evaluation process can be more complex. Commercial properties, such as office buildings or retail spaces, depend heavily on the strength of the local economy and the demand for space in that market. Researching the area's commercial growth potential is critical—are new businesses opening in the area? Is there infrastructure development that could boost the demand for commercial properties? Thoroughly analyzing these factors will help you make a better-informed decision.

It's also important to factor in the condition of the property. A property in good condition will typically require fewer repairs and maintenance, saving you time and money in the long run. However, fixer-upper properties can be a great way to add value and equity quickly, provided you have the time, skills, and budget for renovations. Be realistic about the costs and time involved in fixing up a property—sometimes the potential for higher returns is outweighed by the expenses and effort required to bring a property up to standard.

Another factor to consider is the financial viability of the property. Will the numbers work? That's the big question when evaluating a property. To determine this, you'll need to analyze key metrics like the capitalization rate (cap rate), return on investment (ROI), and cash flow. The cap rate measures the property's potential return based on its net operating income, while ROI helps you understand how much you'll earn relative to the money you've invested. Cash flow refers to the income the property generates after expenses. The goal is to find a property where the rental income exceeds your expenses, generating positive cash flow each month.

Finding the right property also means being patient. It's tempting to rush into a deal, especially if you're eager to get started, but real estate investing is a long game. Rushing into the wrong property can result in costly mistakes, both financially and emotionally. Take your time to carefully analyze each option, and be prepared to walk away from deals that don't meet your criteria.

The search for the right property is an exciting journey, but it requires a mix of research, patience, and strategic thinking. By staying focused on your investment goals, thoroughly evaluating the property's potential, and considering factors like location, condition, and financial viability, you'll be well on your way to finding a property that not only fits your current needs but also positions you for long-term success. Every great investor knows that the key to success in real estate is not about buying just any property—it's about buying the right property. And with the right approach, that perfect investment opportunity is just around the corner.

How to Choose a Profitable Market

The secret to a successful real estate investment is often rooted in one simple truth: location, location, location. Understanding how to choose the right market is crucial for ensuring that your investment yields long-term returns. Picking a profitable market involves more than just choosing a city or neighborhood at random; it's about carefully analyzing different factors that can impact the demand for properties and the potential for rental income.

Start by conducting thorough **market research**. Look for areas that show signs of growth, both in terms of property value and demand for rentals. This might include neighborhoods that are undergoing gentrification or regions with growing job markets. Cities with expanding industries, universities, or tech hubs tend to have strong demand for both rentals and properties for sale, making them ideal places to invest. Pay attention to **economic indicators** such as job growth, population growth, and new business developments. These factors often signal a growing market where rental demand and property values are on the rise.

Proximity to essential amenities is another important factor in selecting a profitable market. **Schools, shopping centers, public transport, and hospitals** are key amenities that tenants look for when renting a property. For example, family-oriented buyers and renters often prioritize school districts, so properties near top-rated schools can appreciate in value over time. Similarly, young professionals may be attracted to urban locations with easy access to nightlife, restaurants, and public transportation.

Another factor to consider is property prices and rent trends. In many cases, a profitable market isn't just about high appreciation rates but also a strong rental demand. A good rule of thumb is to look for markets where the rental income can comfortably cover the cost of owning the property, including mortgage payments, taxes, maintenance, and property management fees. Websites like Zillow, Realtor.com, and local property listing sites can help you track these trends and see if the numbers work in your favor.

Evaluating Property Types: Residential, Commercial, and More

When selecting a property, it's important to understand the differences between property types and how they fit into your investment strategy. The two most common types of properties—**residential and commercial**—each have unique characteristics that can significantly affect your cash flow, potential returns, and the level of involvement you'll have in the management of the property.

Residential properties are often the easiest for new investors to get into. These include single-family homes, multi-family buildings, and condos. Residential properties typically offer more predictable rental income, as people always need a place to live. With a single-family home, for example, you can generate passive income by renting it out to a family or individual. However, you'll need to consider factors like tenant turnover rates, maintenance costs, and the local demand for rental housing.

On the other hand, **commercial properties** (office buildings, retail spaces, industrial warehouses) can yield higher returns, but they come with their own set of challenges. Commercial tenants typically sign longer leases, providing more stability in rental income. However, these properties often come with higher upfront costs and require more extensive market knowledge. Commercial properties also require more management, as businesses may need special accommodations or improvements. Commercial real estate also tends to be more cyclical, with market conditions impacting property values based on demand for commercial space. In contrast, residential properties tend to be more stable since the need for housing is less affected by economic cycles.

A less conventional property type that is gaining popularity among investors is **mixed-use properties**—buildings that combine both residential and commercial units. These can be an attractive option if you want the benefits of both markets, as they provide the opportunity for steady rental income from both residential tenants and commercial businesses. However, managing such a property requires careful attention to both types of tenants, as their needs and concerns will differ.

What Makes a Good Investment Property

When evaluating potential investment properties, there are several characteristics that make a property a good long-term investment. A key factor is **cash flow.** A good investment property will generate consistent rental income that exceeds your monthly expenses. This includes not just your mortgage payment but also taxes, insurance, repairs, and property management fees. Ideally, you want your property to have positive cash flow from day one.

Appreciation is another key element. Over time, properties typically increase in value, especially in markets with strong demand and growing economies. While appreciation isn't guaranteed, selecting properties in **up-and-coming neighborhoods** or areas with economic growth can increase the likelihood of substantial value growth over time.

Another consideration is the **condition of the property.** Properties that are in good condition or require minimal repairs tend to offer more immediate returns. However, if you're willing to put in the work, **fixer-uppers** can offer great opportunities for increasing value quickly. If you decide to go this route, it's important to carefully assess the cost of renovations and ensure that the potential return on investment justifies the time and money spent.

The **neighborhood** where the property is located can be just as important as the property itself. Look for areas that are either already thriving or showing signs of potential. Areas with ongoing infrastructure development, such as new roads, public transportation lines, or commercial projects, can significantly boost property values. A neighborhood that has access to good schools, healthcare, and shopping is more likely to attract tenants and buyers, ensuring a steady stream of rental income and eventual resale value.

It's also essential to consider the **market competition.** How many similar properties are in the area, and what are they renting or selling for? A good investment property will have relatively little competition in terms of price and rental demand. This is especially true for multi-family units—where a lack of similar units can make your property stand out in a crowded market.

Finally, think about your **exit strategy.** A good investment property should offer flexibility in terms of future sale or refinancing options. Ideally, you want a property that you can hold onto for the long term, but if you need to sell it in the future, you want to make sure that it will be easy to move quickly and at a profit. Understanding the local market, having a clear plan, and being ready to adapt to changing conditions can help make any property a good long-term investment.

Finding the right property isn't always about getting lucky—it's about understanding the factors that make a property valuable and aligning them with your investment goals. Whether you're looking for residential, commercial, or mixed-use properties, carefully evaluating these factors will help you choose a profitable investment that sets you up for success. With the right research, patience, and strategy, you can find a property that not only suits your needs but also provides lasting financial benefits.

Chapter 4: Analyzing Potential Returns

"Don't work for money, make money work for you." — Robert Kiyosaki

When it comes to investing in real estate, understanding your potential returns is key to ensuring the investment is worth your time and effort. Whether you're purchasing a single-family home or a large commercial property, knowing how to analyze returns will determine whether or not you're on the path to financial success. But how do you measure a good investment, and what numbers should you be looking at to make sure your decision pays off in the long run?

Real estate investing isn't a "get rich quick" game; it's a long-term strategy that requires careful thought, precise calculations, and constant monitoring of your assets. The first step in analyzing potential returns is understanding the concept of cash flow—how much money you'll actually put in your pocket after expenses. This is the difference between what you earn in rent and what you spend on things like mortgage payments, property taxes, insurance, and maintenance costs. The more cash flow you have, the greater your ability to reinvest, pay down debt, or simply build wealth.

While cash flow is an essential part of your return, you also need to consider **capital appreciation**—the increase in value of the property over time. Unlike stocks or other investments that may fluctuate wildly, real estate tends to appreciate steadily, especially in well-chosen markets. This means that, in addition to the money you make each month from renting out the property, your investment can also grow in value, allowing you to sell it for a profit down the line.

The next critical factor in analyzing returns is the **rate of return on investment (ROI)**. ROI is a percentage that tells you how much you stand to earn compared to how much you've invested. To calculate ROI, you'll first need to figure out the **total cost of your investment,** including the purchase price, closing costs, renovation expenses, and any other costs incurred during the acquisition process. Once you have the total investment, you can calculate ROI by dividing your annual net profit by your total investment, then multiplying that number by 100. A higher ROI indicates a more profitable investment.

Another key metric to measure is the **capitalization rate (cap rate),** which is used to evaluate the profitability of income-generating properties. The cap rate gives you an idea of the return you can expect on a property based on its net operating income (NOI), without taking into account financing costs. It's calculated by dividing the property's annual net operating income by its current market value. A higher cap rate typically indicates a higher potential return, though it may also reflect higher risk. Ideally, you want to find a property with a cap rate that offers a good balance between risk and reward.

Don't forget about **equity**—the portion of the property that you own outright. As you pay down your mortgage, your equity in the property increases, and over time, this can contribute to your overall returns. Your equity is essentially the difference between the current value of the property and what you still owe on it. The more equity you build, the better positioned you'll be to leverage that property for future investments or sell it for a large profit.

Analyzing potential returns isn't just about looking at a few key numbers—it's about understanding the full picture of how your investment will work for you over time. Beyond the standard metrics, take into account the local market conditions and the potential for future growth. Will the neighborhood continue to develop, and are there plans for infrastructure improvements that could increase the property's value?

What does the rental demand look like, and will it be sustainable?

Ultimately, the goal is to find properties that offer both short-term income and long-term appreciation, giving you multiple avenues for growth and financial stability. The more you know about how to evaluate these returns, the better you'll be at making sound decisions that will benefit your financial future for years to come. By using a combination of these tools and techniques, you'll have a clear picture of your investment's potential and will be ready to take the next steps toward building long-term wealth through real estate.

The Numbers You Need to Know

When evaluating the profitability of an investment property, the key to making informed decisions lies in understanding the numbers. Investors need to evaluate various financial metrics that reflect the true performance of a property, from cash flow to return on investment (ROI). Knowing these numbers will not only help you determine if a property is worth purchasing but will also guide you in comparing different properties to identify the best opportunities. Let's break down the core numbers that every investor must be familiar with.

One of the most crucial metrics in evaluating real estate profitability is cash flow. Cash flow is the money you earn from the property after all operating expenses have been paid. It's important because it represents your actual earnings from the investment on a monthly or yearly basis. To calculate cash flow, you'll subtract all expenses from your rental income, including mortgage payments, property taxes, insurance, maintenance costs, and any management fees. The formula looks like this:

Cash Flow = Rental Income - Operating Expenses

For example, if your property generates $2,500 in monthly rent and your monthly expenses total $2,000 (including mortgage, taxes, maintenance, etc.), your monthly cash flow would be:

$2,500 (income) - $2,000 (expenses) = $500 (cash flow)

This positive cash flow indicates that the property is earning money after expenses. A negative cash flow, however, would suggest that you are losing money each month, which can be a red flag for investors unless you have a strategy in place for covering the deficit, such as appreciation or tax breaks.

How to Calculate Cash Flow and ROI

Understanding cash flow is essential, but you must also evaluate the Return on Investment (ROI) to understand the long-term potential of your property. ROI is a percentage that reflects the efficiency of your investment. It is calculated by dividing your annual net profit (after expenses) by your total investment (including the property purchase price, closing costs, and renovation expenses), then multiplying that figure by 100. The formula is:

ROI = (Annual Profit / Total Investment) x 100

Let's look at an example. Suppose you invested $200,000 in a property, and after all expenses (mortgage, repairs, taxes, etc.), you earn $12,000 annually in net profit. To calculate the ROI:

ROI = ($12,000 / $200,000) x 100 = 6%

An ROI of 6% is considered a solid return for a real estate investment. However, the ideal ROI can vary based on market conditions, risk tolerance, and your investment goals. Generally, investors aim for a minimum ROI of 8-12% for rental properties, though this can fluctuate depending on the property type and location.

Another important metric in assessing potential returns is the capitalization rate (cap rate). This metric gives you an idea of the rate of return you can expect on a property based on its net operating income (NOI). Cap rate is calculated by dividing the property's annual NOI by its purchase price. The formula is:

Cap Rate = Annual NOI / Property Purchase Price

For example, if a property generates $20,000 annually in net operating income and costs $250,000, the cap rate would be:

Cap Rate = $20,000 / $250,000 = 0.08 or 8%

A higher cap rate typically indicates a more profitable property, but it may also suggest higher risk. Lower cap rates are often seen in more stable, lower-risk markets, while higher cap rates may indicate emerging markets or properties that need more work.

Using Comparative Market Analysis (CMA)

While cash flow, ROI, and cap rate are important, no investment decision should be made without understanding how the property compares to others in the market. A Comparative Market Analysis (CMA) is a tool that helps you evaluate the value of a property based on recent sales of similar properties in the area. A CMA will consider the property's size, location, condition, and other factors that influence its value. This analysis can help you determine if a property is priced fairly and whether it's a good deal compared to other properties available in the market.

For example, if you're considering purchasing a two-bedroom house in a neighborhood where similar homes have recently sold for $180,000 to $200,000, and you find a similar property listed for $220,000, you might want to proceed with caution. This price could be inflated, or there may be issues with the property that justify a lower sale price.

Real-Life Example:

Let's look at a real-world example of how these metrics play out. Suppose you're considering a single-family home that costs $300,000. The property generates $2,500 in monthly rent, which gives you an annual rental income of $30,000. Your operating expenses total $18,000 annually (including mortgage, taxes, insurance, and maintenance costs), leaving you with $12,000 in net income.

Your cash flow would be $12,000, which is your annual profit after all expenses. Next, calculate your ROI:

ROI = ($12,000 / $300,000) x 100 = 4%

Next, calculate the cap rate:

Cap Rate = $12,000 / $300,000 = 4%

The cash flow, ROI, and cap rate give you a good indication of the property's performance. However, to really dig deeper, you would use a CMA to check that the $300,000 asking price aligns with comparable properties in the area. If similar homes are selling for around $280,000, then you may have some room to negotiate.

These numbers give you a solid framework to evaluate an investment property and make informed decisions about your portfolio. By using these metrics, you can confidently assess whether the property is a good fit for your investment strategy. Whether you're just getting started or looking to expand your portfolio, understanding how to measure returns and evaluate profitability is key to real estate investing success.

Chapter 5: Financing Your Investment

"Real estate is not just about property. It's about people and the financial systems that make it possible to build wealth."

One of the most exciting yet daunting aspects of real estate investing is finding the right financing options. Whether you're looking to purchase your first investment property or expand your portfolio, understanding the various ways to finance your real estate ventures is crucial. Unlike stocks or bonds, where investments can often be made with relatively small amounts of capital, real estate typically requires a significant initial outlay. But, the right financing can unlock opportunities that may have otherwise been out of reach, allowing you to take that first step toward building long-term wealth.

First and foremost, it's important to recognize that securing financing is not a one-size-fits-all process. There are many different methods to fund a real estate investment, and your decision will depend on factors such as your financial situation, the type of property you're purchasing, your long-term goals, and the market conditions. Conventional mortgages, private loans, hard money loans, and even partnerships are all potential sources of funding, each with its pros and cons.

A traditional mortgage is the most common method for financing a property purchase. These loans, offered by banks or other lenders, usually require a down payment of at least 20% of the property's purchase price. For a $300,000 property, that means you'd need to have $60,000 upfront. The advantage of traditional mortgages is that they often come with lower interest rates and longer repayment terms, typically 15 to 30 years, making them a solid choice for long-term investors. However, qualifying for a conventional mortgage can be challenging, particularly for first-time buyers or those without a strong credit history. Lenders will scrutinize your income, credit score, debt-to-income ratio, and other factors to determine whether you qualify.

If you're unable to secure a traditional loan, there are alternative financing methods worth considering. Private loans from family, friends, or individual investors can be a viable option, particularly for those looking to bypass the often rigid requirements of traditional lenders. Private loans may offer more flexibility, but they also come with their own risks, especially when borrowing from people you have personal relationships with. Setting clear terms and agreements is essential to avoid misunderstandings or damaged relationships.

Another option for financing your investment is hard money loans, which are typically offered by private lenders or investors. These loans are short-term and backed by the property itself, which means they come with higher interest rates and shorter repayment terms than conventional loans. They can be a good option for real estate investors looking to quickly purchase and renovate a property before selling it or refinancing into a more favorable loan. However, these loans should be approached with caution, as their high costs can eat into potential profits if you don't manage your investment wisely.

For those looking to pool resources, partnerships are a popular option. By partnering with other investors, you can leverage their financial strength and resources to secure the capital needed to invest in properties that would otherwise be out of reach. Partnerships can take many forms, from informal agreements between friends and family members to more formal joint ventures. The key to a successful partnership is clear communication and a shared vision of the investment's goals. It's also important to have a legal agreement in place that outlines each partner's role, contribution, and share of the profits.

Beyond securing financing, it's equally important to be mindful of closing costs, which can quickly add up and eat into your budget. These costs typically include property inspection fees, title insurance, attorney fees, and recording fees, among others. On average, closing costs can range from 2% to 5% of the purchase price. So, for a $300,000 property, you could be looking at an additional $6,000 to $15,000 in expenses. Budgeting for these costs ahead of time will ensure that you're not caught off guard when the deal is about to close.

Regardless of how you choose to finance your real estate investment, it's essential to do your due diligence. Understanding the terms and conditions of your financing, the potential risks, and how the investment aligns with your long-term goals is key to ensuring that you make a sound decision. By carefully weighing your options, you'll be better prepared to navigate the complexities of real estate investing and position yourself for success in the long run. The right financing could be the very thing that turns your real estate aspirations into tangible financial gains.

Traditional Financing vs. Alternative Methods

When it comes to financing a real estate investment, beginners often find themselves at a crossroads: Should they pursue conventional financing or explore alternative options? Both paths offer unique advantages and challenges, and understanding the differences can help you make a more informed decision as you navigate the complex world of real estate.

Conventional financing, particularly traditional mortgages, is the most well-known option for most real estate investors. A conventional mortgage is a loan provided by a bank, credit union, or mortgage lender, typically requiring a down payment of 20% of the property's purchase price. These loans often come with relatively low interest rates and longer repayment terms—15 to 30 years—which make them an attractive choice for long-term investors looking to build a stable portfolio. However, securing a traditional mortgage requires a strong credit score, a stable income, and a low debt-to-income ratio. This can be a barrier for new investors who are just starting out and may not have the credit history or financial track record to meet the lender's requirements.

For those who may not qualify for a conventional mortgage or prefer more flexible terms, alternative financing methods can provide viable solutions. One popular alternative is the hard money loan, which is typically offered by private investors or companies rather than banks. Hard money loans are short-term loans secured by the property itself, and they generally come with higher interest rates—sometimes as much as 10% to 15%. The advantage of hard money loans is that they are easier and quicker to obtain than traditional mortgages, and they don't rely as heavily on your credit score. This makes them a suitable option for real estate investors looking to purchase properties in need of renovation or those who plan to flip properties quickly.

Another alternative is crowdfunding, which has become increasingly popular in recent years. Real estate crowdfunding allows individuals to pool their money together online to invest in properties that they might not have been able to afford individually. This method is particularly appealing to beginners because it often requires a relatively small minimum investment, and investors can diversify their portfolios by investing in multiple projects. However, like hard money loans, crowdfunding comes with risks—especially in terms of the lack of liquidity and the potential for market volatility.

Each of these financing methods offers different benefits and drawbacks, so the key to success is understanding your investment goals, financial situation, and risk tolerance. By evaluating the pros and cons of each option, you can determine which financing method best aligns with your long-term objectives.

Understanding Mortgages, Loans, and Down Payments

At the heart of any traditional real estate financing is the mortgage. A mortgage is simply a loan that's secured by the property you intend to purchase. When you take out a mortgage, you agree to pay back the lender over a specified period—usually between 15 and 30 years—with interest. The interest rate you're offered depends on various factors, including your credit score, the type of loan, and market conditions. Fixed-rate mortgages have an interest rate that remains the same for the life of the loan, while adjustable-rate mortgages (ARMs) can change after a certain period, often resulting in lower initial payments but potential fluctuations in the future.

One of the most important aspects of securing a mortgage is the down payment. A down payment is the upfront amount you pay toward the purchase of a property, and it is typically expressed as a percentage of the purchase price. For conventional loans, the down payment is usually 20%, although there are government-backed loans (such as FHA loans) that require as little as 3.5% down. The larger your down payment, the less you'll need to borrow, which can result in lower monthly payments and less interest paid over the life of the loan.

Understanding loan terms is another critical component of financing. Loan terms refer to the length of time you have to repay the loan. For example, a 30-year mortgage means you'll have 30 years to pay off the loan. Shorter loan terms generally come with higher monthly payments but lower overall interest costs. It's important to weigh your monthly budget against your long-term financial goals to decide on the best loan term for your situation.

When evaluating loans, you should also consider interest rates, which can vary widely depending on market conditions and the type of loan you're securing. A lower interest rate can save you thousands of dollars over the life of your loan, so it's essential to shop around for the best deal. Additionally, some loans come with prepayment penalties, which can add extra costs if you decide to pay off your mortgage early.

Creative Financing Options for Beginners

For those who may not want to go the traditional route or are looking for more creative ways to finance their investments, there are several innovative options worth considering. Seller financing is one such strategy, where the seller acts as the lender and you make payments directly to them instead of going through a bank. This can be particularly useful if you have trouble qualifying for a traditional loan, as it allows for more flexible terms. However, seller financing typically requires a larger down payment, and interest rates may be higher than those of traditional mortgages.

Another option is lease options, where you lease a property with the option to purchase it later. This can be an excellent choice for beginners who want to test the waters of real estate investing without committing to the full purchase price upfront. Lease options often come with the advantage of locking in a future purchase price, which can be beneficial if the property's value appreciates over time.

For those looking to partner with others, partnerships and joint ventures can offer a way to pool resources and share risks. If you have limited capital but access to expertise, a partnership can allow you to leverage your strengths and invest in larger, more profitable properties. In these situations, clear agreements should be made upfront regarding each partner's role, contributions, and share of the profits.

Finally, home equity loans and lines of credit (HELOCs) are also creative ways to finance real estate investments. If you already own a home with significant equity, you can use that equity to secure financing for an investment property. These options can offer lower interest rates compared to other methods, but they come with the risk of losing your primary home if you fail to repay the loan.

Whichever financing route you choose, it's important to ensure that you are financially prepared. Take the time to assess your credit, save for a down payment, and carefully consider your financing options before making a commitment. Each financing option has its benefits, and the key to successful real estate investing is choosing the one that aligns with your financial situation, investment goals, and risk tolerance.

Chapter 6: Managing Your Property

"A good property manager is worth their weight in gold."

This quote is a reminder that managing real estate investments requires more than just owning property—it takes time, effort, and strategic thinking to ensure your investments thrive. Whether you're a seasoned investor with a large portfolio or just getting started with your first property, learning the ropes of property management is a critical step toward success. In this chapter, we'll dive into what it takes to effectively manage your property, reduce headaches, and maximize your return on investment.

Managing property goes beyond collecting rent checks. It's about maintaining the value of the property, ensuring a steady cash flow, and creating positive experiences for tenants. From finding the right tenants to handling day-to-day maintenance, a proactive approach can save you both time and money. The first step to successful property management is understanding the key responsibilities involved. This includes property upkeep, managing tenant relationships, handling lease agreements, and ensuring timely rent payments.

One of the first decisions you'll face is whether to manage your property yourself or hire a property management company. For new investors, managing a property on your own can be a great way to learn the ins and outs of the business and save on management fees. However, it can also be time-consuming and challenging, especially when it comes to handling maintenance issues, tenant complaints, or legal requirements. A property management company, on the other hand, can take care of these responsibilities for you, handling everything from tenant screening to routine maintenance, but at a cost—typically 8-12% of the monthly rent.

Regardless of whether you decide to self-manage or hire a professional, it's essential to create a system for handling tenant interactions. Screening tenants is one of the most important aspects of property management. A thorough screening process helps ensure that you're renting to responsible individuals who will pay rent on time, take care of the property, and respect the terms of the lease. This involves checking references, verifying income, running background and credit checks, and interviewing potential tenants.

Once you've found the right tenants, clear communication is key to a successful relationship. Setting expectations from the start, such as outlining rules in the lease agreement and maintaining open lines of communication, can prevent many problems down the road. If you're self-managing, having a reliable method of collecting rent and addressing tenant inquiries is essential. This could be through online portals, phone, or email—whichever system works best for both you and your tenants.

Another vital aspect of property management is regular property maintenance. Keeping up with routine maintenance tasks—such as HVAC servicing, plumbing checks, and landscaping—can prevent costly repairs in the future and keep your tenants satisfied. A well-maintained property is not only more attractive to tenants but also holds its value better over time. Having a network of trusted contractors or a local handyman can ensure you have quick solutions for any issues that arise.

In addition to maintenance, staying on top of legal and financial responsibilities is crucial. As a property owner, you'll need to comply with landlord-tenant laws, which can vary by state or country. This includes respecting tenants' rights, adhering to fair housing laws, and handling security deposits correctly. On the financial side, keeping track of income and expenses, paying taxes, and budgeting for repairs and upgrades ensures that your property is financially viable.

Managing a property may seem daunting at first, but with the right knowledge and systems in place, it can be one of the most rewarding aspects of real estate investing. Whether you choose to manage the property yourself or hire a professional, being proactive, organized, and communicative will help you maintain happy tenants, ensure consistent rental income, and ultimately, protect and grow your investment. The key to success is staying engaged with your property, addressing issues before they become problems, and consistently working to improve both the tenant experience and the value of the property itself.

The Basics of Property Management

Property management is the backbone of real estate investing, ensuring that your investment generates steady income and appreciates over time. But it's more than just collecting rent every month. A successful property manager—whether that's you or a hired professional—must juggle several roles: financial manager, customer service representative, maintenance coordinator, and legal expert. At its core, property management involves overseeing the day-to-day operations of your property, which includes handling tenant relations, property maintenance, lease enforcement, and financial management.

A well-managed property ensures that your tenants are happy, your property is well-maintained, and your financial goals are being met. Rent collection is a crucial part of this process. Setting clear terms for rent payments, such as due dates, penalties for late payments, and preferred payment methods, can significantly reduce headaches down the road. It's also essential to stay on top of tenant communication—whether it's regarding maintenance requests, inquiries, or complaints. Proactive communication prevents misunderstandings and helps keep the property running smoothly.

Equally important is staying organized with the financial side of things. Keeping track of rental income, maintenance costs, property taxes, and insurance premiums ensures that your investment remains profitable. The financial management aspect also extends to budgeting for unforeseen repairs or vacancies, which are part of the real estate business. Overall, good property management is a blend of attention to detail, proactive communication, and a thorough understanding of your legal and financial obligations as a landlord.

How to Find and Screen Tenants

Finding the right tenants is perhaps the most critical aspect of property management. Tenants who pay rent on time, take care of the property, and follow the lease terms will make your life much easier. The first step is marketing your property. Make sure your listings are clear, accurate, and appealing. High-quality photos and detailed descriptions will attract serious inquiries.

Once you begin receiving applications, screening tenants carefully is key. Tenant screening helps minimize the risk of renting to someone who may cause problems down the road. Start by reviewing the application for completeness, then proceed with background checks, credit reports, and income verification. A solid tenant should have a steady income that covers the rent, a decent credit score that suggests financial responsibility, and a clean background check.

References from previous landlords are incredibly valuable. Speak to former property managers to gauge whether the applicant had a history of paying rent on time and maintaining the property. Additionally, conduct an interview with the potential tenant to assess their communication skills and personality. This gives you an idea of whether they'll be a good fit for your property and whether they're someone you can easily work with if issues arise.

Remember, while it's important to find tenants who meet your criteria, it's also critical to comply with fair housing laws. Never discriminate against potential tenants based on race, gender, religion, or other protected categories. Your goal should always be to find the best candidate who will respect your property and the terms of the lease.

Maintenance, Repairs, and Legal Responsibilities

A significant part of property management is ensuring the property remains in good condition. Regular maintenance and prompt repairs are vital for keeping tenants satisfied and preventing small issues from becoming major problems. Routine tasks, such as cleaning gutters, servicing HVAC systems, and ensuring plumbing and electrical systems are functioning, should be part of your regular schedule. Staying on top of maintenance helps preserve the value of your investment and avoid expensive emergency repairs.

In addition to routine maintenance, being prepared for unexpected repairs is also essential. A leaking roof, broken appliance, or malfunctioning water heater can cause significant tenant dissatisfaction and may even lead to legal complications. Having a list of trusted contractors or repairmen to call on for quick service is key. You can also consider implementing an online system for tenants to submit maintenance requests, which can help you track issues and respond in a timely manner.

Legal responsibilities play a major role in property management. As a landlord, you must understand and follow local and national housing laws. These regulations cover various areas, such as eviction processes, handling security deposits, and ensuring the property is habitable. For example, most states have strict rules about how and when you can evict a tenant for non-payment of rent, and these rules must be followed to the letter to avoid legal consequences.

Security deposits are another important legal aspect. They are typically collected before a tenant moves in and are meant to cover any damages or unpaid rent when the tenant moves out. It's essential to know how much you can legally charge for a deposit and how you're required to handle it once the tenant moves out. Many states require landlords to provide an itemized list of deductions if part of the deposit is withheld.

For those who opt to self-manage, understanding these legalities is crucial to avoid costly mistakes. If you don't feel confident in your legal knowledge, consider seeking advice from a real estate attorney or hiring a property management company to handle these responsibilities.

Property management is both an art and a science. Effective management requires staying organized, being responsive to tenant needs, keeping up with legal responsibilities, and maintaining the property in a way that protects its value. Whether you choose to manage your property yourself or hire a professional, being hands-on in the process and knowing what to look out for can make the difference between a successful investment and a frustrating one. The better you manage your property, the greater your chances of achieving long-term financial success.

Chapter 7: Minimizing Risk and Maximizing Profit

"Risk comes from not knowing what you're doing." – Warren Buffett

In real estate, risk is an inherent part of the game, but it doesn't have to dictate your success. Every decision you make as an investor has the potential to either minimize or escalate your risk, and understanding how to navigate these risks is the key to maximizing your profits. By making strategic choices and preparing for the unexpected, you can protect your investments and position yourself for long-term success.

The first step in minimizing risk is choosing the right property and the right location. A property in a high-demand area with a stable economy, low crime rates, and good infrastructure is far less risky than one in a declining neighborhood. The potential for consistent rental income is much higher in locations where demand outstrips supply.

Additionally, researching the local economy and real estate market trends can give you a sense of the area's future prospects. While no location is entirely risk-free, doing your homework can significantly reduce the chances of unexpected financial hardship.

Another way to minimize risk is by diversifying your real estate portfolio. Relying on a single property, or even a single type of property, can leave you vulnerable to market fluctuations, tenant turnover, or unforeseen maintenance issues. By investing in different types of properties—residential, commercial, or even vacation rentals—you can spread your risk. This strategy not only protects you from downturns in one specific market segment but also provides opportunities for growth across various sectors.

A key part of reducing risk is having the right insurance in place. Property insurance, liability coverage, and rental insurance can help mitigate financial loss from disasters, tenant damages, or lawsuits. Insurance might seem like an additional expense, but when a natural disaster strikes or if a tenant sues you for an injury on your property, it will be worth every penny. Make sure to review your policy regularly to ensure that it covers any potential risks your investment may face.

Another risk management strategy is ensuring that you have sufficient cash flow. Emergencies can happen, and having a financial buffer to cover vacancies, maintenance, or market downturns can save you from scrambling when challenges arise. Property investors often overlook the importance of creating an emergency fund, but this safety net can make all the difference in how smoothly your investment performs over time.

When it comes to maximizing profit, there are several strategies you can adopt. One of the most effective ways to increase returns is to add value to the property. Simple improvements, like updating appliances, landscaping, or adding a fresh coat of paint, can increase the value of your property and attract higher-paying tenants. When tenants see value in the property, they are more likely to stay longer, pay rent on time, and respect the property.

Furthermore, rental income can be maximized by strategically pricing your property. Overpricing can lead to vacancies, while underpricing may lead to lost profit. Researching comparable properties in the area (known as "comps") will help you find a sweet spot for rent pricing. Seasonal fluctuations can also play a role in pricing strategy. For example, in vacation rental markets, demand tends to spike during peak seasons, which presents an opportunity to increase rates during high-demand periods.

One of the smartest ways to maximize profit is by leveraging financing. Taking out a mortgage or loan allows you to control a large asset with a relatively small initial investment. While borrowing money carries the risk of paying interest and potentially overextending yourself financially, it can lead to a higher return on investment (ROI) if the property generates more income than the cost of the loan. This is why it's essential to carefully analyze your potential returns and use leverage wisely.

Lastly, maintaining a good relationship with tenants is not just a matter of tenant satisfaction; it's about maintaining steady cash flow. Keeping communication open, addressing maintenance issues promptly, and respecting your tenants' rights can reduce turnover, minimize vacancies, and ensure that tenants renew their leases. Happy tenants are more likely to stay, which means a consistent income stream for you.

Real estate investing is a balancing act between managing risks and capitalizing on opportunities. By making smart, informed decisions about where to invest, how to finance, and how to manage your properties, you can keep your risks in check while reaping the rewards of your hard work. When approached with strategy, real estate is one of the most rewarding investment vehicles available, providing steady cash flow, long-term wealth, and financial security.

Understanding Market Cycles and Trends

The real estate market doesn't operate in a vacuum; it's highly sensitive to a range of economic, political, and societal forces. One of the most critical aspects of real estate investing is understanding market cycles and trends. Whether you're a seasoned investor or just starting out, the ability to anticipate and respond to market fluctuations is essential for maximizing profits and minimizing risk.

Market cycles typically move through four phases: expansion, peak, contraction, and recovery. During the expansion phase, the market sees increasing demand, rising property values, and low vacancy rates.

However, this phase doesn't last forever. As demand peaks, the market enters the peak phase, where values might be at their highest, but also more volatile. When the economy starts to slow down or interest rates rise, the market enters the contraction phase, where property values begin to fall, and vacancy rates rise. Finally, the recovery phase is when prices stabilize, and the market starts to grow again. Understanding where we are in the cycle can help you make informed decisions about buying, holding, or selling properties.

But it's not just about recognizing broad market cycles. Local market conditions also play a pivotal role in determining when and where to invest. Look at factors such as job growth, population trends, infrastructure development, and changes in local government policies. These are often leading indicators of future property demand. For instance, a new university or corporate headquarters opening nearby could signal a surge in housing demand.

By staying informed about national and local market conditions, you can avoid investing at the wrong time, such as buying during the peak phase when prices are inflated. Additionally, regularly monitoring market trends allows you to make adjustments to your portfolio to maximize returns or protect yourself from a downturn. The key is not just reacting to market changes but anticipating them as much as possible.

How to Mitigate Risks in Property Investment

Real estate investing comes with its fair share of risks. The market may be unpredictable, tenant issues can arise, and even the best-laid plans may go awry. However, understanding these risks and employing strategies to mitigate them can help ensure that your investments remain profitable even in less-than-ideal conditions.

One of the most significant risks in real estate investing is market downturns. Economic recessions, rising interest rates, or other unforeseen events can cause property values to drop, leading to negative equity. To mitigate this risk, diversification is key. By investing in a mix of property types (residential, commercial, industrial) and geographical locations, you spread your exposure to various market conditions. Diversifying ensures that if one market takes a downturn, you have other investments that can weather the storm.

Tenant-related issues are another risk that can disrupt your returns. Late payments, high turnover rates, and property damage caused by tenants are all common challenges. To minimize this risk, thorough tenant screening is essential. Conduct background checks, credit checks, and verify references before signing a lease agreement. Additionally, having a solid lease in place that clearly outlines tenants' responsibilities can help prevent conflicts. For higher-risk tenants, consider asking for a larger security deposit or requiring renters' insurance.

Insurance is a powerful tool for mitigating physical risks. Adequate property insurance, including liability and renter's insurance, ensures that you're covered in case of damage to the property or lawsuits arising from tenant injuries. It's worth investing in the right level of coverage, especially when it comes to natural disasters or extreme weather conditions that might affect your area.

Proper legal protections also play a vital role in risk management. Familiarizing yourself with local landlord-tenant laws, zoning regulations, and eviction procedures can help you avoid legal trouble. Many investors hire property managers or legal advisors to ensure they are fully compliant with all local laws. In addition, incorporating your investment property into a limited liability company (LLC) can protect your personal assets from any legal claims that arise related to your property.

Strategies for Increasing Property Value

The value of your property is largely determined by the market, but there are several strategies you can employ to increase its value over time. Adding value to a property through renovations or improvements can significantly enhance your return on investment, especially in a competitive market.

Renovations can range from simple cosmetic updates like fresh paint and new flooring to more significant renovations such as kitchen remodels or bathroom upgrades. The key is to focus on improvements that have the most impact in your specific market. In areas where rental demand is high, modernizing kitchens or bathrooms can attract tenants willing to pay a premium for upgraded finishes. Even small touches, like new light fixtures or landscaping, can make a difference in the property's overall appeal.

Strategic improvements can also boost the property's long-term value. For example, if you own a multifamily property, consider adding amenities like a washer/dryer in-unit, upgraded security systems, or parking spaces. These types of improvements not only increase the appeal of your property but also help in retaining tenants, reducing turnover, and ultimately increasing cash flow.

If you're looking to invest in a commercial property, you might focus on improvements that increase the building's energy efficiency. Features like solar panels, high-efficiency heating and cooling systems, or better insulation can significantly reduce operating costs for tenants and make your property more attractive to businesses looking to minimize overhead.

Aside from physical upgrades, increasing the property's value also involves improving its financial performance. This could mean raising rents in line with market rates, reducing vacancy periods, or making the property more attractive to higher-paying tenants. Regularly reassess the rent and keep it aligned with local market conditions. A well-maintained property with high tenant satisfaction often results in longer leases, fewer vacancies, and ultimately a stronger return on investment.

Lastly, conducting due diligence before making any purchase is one of the most effective strategies to protect against financial risk. Researching the property's history, condition, local market conditions, and potential for future growth ensures that you make an informed decision. Don't rely solely on the seller's word or the property's aesthetic appeal. A comprehensive assessment will help you identify hidden issues that may affect the property's value or your ability to rent it out.

Real estate investment, while profitable, requires diligence, patience, and a long-term outlook. By understanding market cycles, reducing risks through diversification and legal protections, and strategically increasing property value, you can create a portfolio that stands the test of time.

Chapter 8: Scaling Your Real Estate Portfolio

"The secret to building wealth is not to make money, but to keep it and grow it."

As you take your first steps into real estate investing, your focus may be primarily on finding that perfect property, managing it effectively, and securing steady cash flow. But the ultimate goal for most investors is not just to maintain a single property but to scale a profitable real estate portfolio. Scaling is the key to unlocking substantial wealth and financial independence, but it requires a strategic mindset, careful planning, and the willingness to take calculated risks.

When it comes to scaling your real estate portfolio, the biggest challenge for many investors is knowing when to expand and how to fund that expansion. You've built the foundation with one or a few properties, but you'll need to leverage your existing assets and explore new avenues of funding to continue growing. In fact, leveraging your existing portfolio is one of the most effective strategies for scaling.

A strong, profitable property portfolio can provide you with the equity needed to purchase additional properties. This concept is referred to as "leveraging," and it's an essential tool for expanding your holdings without depleting your savings. Essentially, you can use the equity in one property as collateral to secure a loan for another. This not only accelerates the process of scaling but allows you to grow faster than if you were solely relying on cash savings.

While leveraging is a powerful tool, it's also crucial to maintain a balance between debt and equity. Over-leveraging can lead to financial strain if rental income does not meet expectations or if property values drop unexpectedly. As your portfolio grows, ensuring that each property generates positive cash flow is vital to avoid cash shortages. Be mindful of your debt-to-income ratio and carefully assess each property's income potential before making the leap to your next purchase.

Another important factor when scaling your real estate investments is managing your time effectively. The more properties you acquire, the more time-consuming your day-to-day responsibilities become. Property management, tenant issues, maintenance, and financing can quickly add up. While you may have started managing a few properties on your own, as you scale, it might make sense to outsource property management. This can free up your time to focus on finding new opportunities and growing your portfolio further.

As your portfolio grows, so too should your knowledge and expertise. Real estate investing is not a "one size fits all" venture. Different markets and types of properties require different strategies. For instance, multi-family units come with distinct considerations compared to single-family homes. Similarly, commercial real estate offers lucrative opportunities but comes with its own set of risks and demands. Expanding into new markets, or investing in different property types, can diversify your portfolio, reduce risk, and increase your profit potential. However, each new venture should come after thorough research and due diligence.

Networking also plays a crucial role in scaling your real estate business. Building relationships with other investors, lenders, real estate agents, and property managers can open doors to more investment opportunities, better deals, and even partnerships. In fact, joint ventures are a common way to scale, especially when you need to pool resources or expertise to take on larger, more complex projects.

The key to scaling your real estate portfolio lies in taking deliberate steps to grow, diversify, and manage risk effectively. When approached thoughtfully, scaling your real estate investments can lead to substantial wealth creation. So, start by leveraging what you have, continue learning, outsource where needed, and always be on the lookout for new opportunities. Building a portfolio that spans multiple properties, markets, and types of real estate can set you on a path to financial freedom and long-term success. The sky's the limit when you know how to scale strategically.

When and How to Expand Your Investments

Scaling your real estate portfolio requires more than just acquiring properties; it's about knowing when the time is right to grow and how to do so strategically. The first step in deciding when to expand is ensuring that the properties you currently own are producing reliable cash flow. Ideally, you should have a clear picture of your financial stability, including the ability to cover mortgage payments, taxes, insurance, and maintenance costs without sacrificing your overall profitability.

Once your initial properties are generating consistent income, you should consider expanding your portfolio. However, scaling doesn't always mean purchasing additional properties immediately. Start by assessing the appreciation potential of your existing properties. If you've built up equity through consistent rent payments or market appreciation, this could be a signal that you're ready to leverage this equity for additional investments.

The best time to scale is when you have access to sufficient equity and when the market conditions are favorable. Expanding during a market boom can offer lucrative opportunities, but be cautious about overextending yourself during a market bubble. On the flip side, some of the best deals are found during down markets when prices are lower. Timing, coupled with diligent market research, can play a significant role in how well your scaling efforts succeed.

The method of expansion also plays a critical role. At first, purchasing single-family homes or duplexes may have seemed like the logical choice. But as your portfolio grows, consider whether expanding into multi-family properties or commercial real estate might be a more efficient way to scale. Multi-family homes, for example, provide more units under one roof, meaning fewer costs per unit, better economies of scale, and less risk than relying on single-family homes.

Using Leverage to Grow Your Portfolio

Leverage is a powerful tool in real estate investing, especially when scaling your portfolio. Simply put, leveraging allows you to use other people's money to increase the potential return on your investment. The most common way investors leverage is by taking out a mortgage on a property. If your existing properties have built up equity, you can use that equity as collateral to secure loans for new properties.

By leveraging existing equity, you don't need to wait until you have the full amount of cash needed to purchase a property. This allows you to acquire more properties, more quickly, and build your portfolio at a faster pace than if you were relying solely on savings. The key here is ensuring that you can handle the debt comfortably. Before using leverage, make sure the properties you are investing in will generate enough income to cover the mortgage payments, property taxes, insurance, and other expenses.

However, leveraging isn't without its risks. The primary risk is over-leveraging, where your debt obligations become so high that a downturn in the market or unexpected expenses put you in a financially precarious position. The goal is to keep your leverage ratio at a manageable level while ensuring that each new property continues to provide a positive cash flow.

Building relationships with partners, co-investors, and lenders is crucial when using leverage. A solid network of people who understand the risks and rewards of real estate investing can provide not only capital but also advice and guidance. Establishing trust with private lenders and financial institutions can open doors to better financing options and better loan terms as you scale.

Diversifying Your Real Estate Holdings

As you scale, diversification should be a central part of your strategy. Diversification involves spreading your investments across different property types, locations, and markets to reduce the risks associated with any single asset. Real estate is cyclical; markets go up, and they go down. By diversifying, you're less likely to suffer a significant loss if one property type or market experiences a downturn.

One way to diversify is by expanding into different types of real estate investments. If you've been focused on residential properties, you might consider commercial real estate or multi-family units. Each type of property comes with its own risk profile and return potential. For instance, commercial properties may offer longer leases and more stable tenants but can come with higher vacancy risks. Multi-family properties often have a lower vacancy risk because even if one tenant leaves, there are others still contributing to your income stream.

Geographical diversification is another important aspect to consider. Rather than investing exclusively in your local market, explore opportunities in other cities or states where prices might be lower, or growth potential is greater. Sometimes, investing in emerging markets can yield higher returns, as properties in these areas have the potential for rapid appreciation. Be mindful of local laws, taxes, and market dynamics before expanding into a new location.

As your portfolio grows, managing a diverse range of properties can become complex. This is where a property management team becomes invaluable. A good property manager can handle the day-to-day responsibilities of each property, leaving you free to focus on finding new investment opportunities. When your properties span across different types of real estate or geographical locations, it's essential to have a reliable system in place to track performance and handle tenant and maintenance issues promptly.

Scaling and diversifying your real estate portfolio requires a balance of strategy, discipline, and a solid understanding of market trends. The more educated and prepared you are, the better equipped you'll be to avoid common scaling mistakes, such as overleveraging or spreading yourself too thin. As you grow, remember that success in real estate isn't just about acquiring more properties—it's about acquiring the right properties and managing them effectively for long-term financial freedom.

Chapter 9: Tax Implications and Benefits

"Real estate is the closest thing to a gold mine." — Robert Kiyosaki

Owning real estate comes with numerous benefits, but understanding the tax implications and benefits of your investments can significantly impact your financial strategy. For many real estate investors, taxes are an area of concern, often seeming complex and daunting. However, once you understand the basics and learn how to take advantage of the tax benefits available to property owners, you'll realize that real estate can be one of the most tax-efficient ways to build wealth.

The first tax benefit most investors encounter is depreciation. Depreciation allows you to deduct the cost of your property over time, which reduces your taxable income. This means that even though the property is likely appreciating in value, the IRS allows you to write off a portion of its value each year. For residential properties, the depreciation period is typically 27.5 years, while commercial properties are depreciated over 39 years. This deduction can significantly reduce the amount of income you report to the IRS, thereby lowering your overall tax liability.

Along with depreciation, there are various deductions available to real estate investors. Mortgage interest is one of the largest deductions available, particularly in the early years of a loan when interest payments make up a large portion of your monthly mortgage. Additionally, operating expenses such as property management fees, repairs and maintenance, insurance premiums, and property taxes can all be deducted from your rental income, helping to offset your earnings.

Another important aspect to consider is the tax treatment of capital gains when you sell a property. If you've owned the property for more than a year, you're typically eligible for long-term capital gains tax rates, which are lower than ordinary income tax rates. However, if you sell a property before the one-year mark, your profits will be taxed as short-term capital gains, which are taxed at a higher rate. Understanding the difference can be vital when planning your exit strategy.

In addition to capital gains tax, investors can benefit from tax deferral strategies, such as the 1031 exchange. A 1031 exchange allows you to sell one property and use the profits to purchase another like-kind property, without paying capital gains taxes in the process. The main benefit here is that you can defer paying taxes on the sale, which allows you to reinvest the profits into a larger or more profitable property. However, there are specific rules and deadlines that must be followed to qualify for this tax benefit, so it's important to consult with a tax professional before proceeding with a 1031 exchange.

Property owners can also benefit from a favorable tax treatment if they hold their property as a rental business. By structuring your investment properly, you may be able to qualify for business deductions, further reducing your taxable income. This might include deducting expenses related to managing your property, such as marketing costs, legal fees, and accounting services.

While there are several tax benefits available to real estate investors, it's equally important to understand the risks and obligations. Real estate taxation is complex, and failing to comply with tax laws can lead to significant penalties. Keeping track of all your expenses, understanding when and how to claim deductions, and working with a qualified tax professional can help you maximize your tax benefits while avoiding any unpleasant surprises from the IRS.

When done correctly, the tax advantages of real estate investing are unparalleled, helping you keep more of your hard-earned money and reinvest it into building a profitable portfolio. Real estate isn't just about cash flow and property appreciation—it's also about tax strategy. Being proactive and informed about your tax obligations and benefits will set you up for long-term success in your real estate ventures.

How Real Estate Investment Affects Your Taxes

Investing in real estate can offer several tax advantages that make it an attractive option for wealth-building. However, real estate investments also come with tax implications that need to be carefully understood and managed. One of the primary tax considerations for real estate investors is rental income. Rental income is considered taxable income, meaning the IRS expects you to report it as part of your earnings. However, this doesn't mean you'll pay taxes on the entire amount. The key to minimizing your tax liability lies in the ability to deduct certain expenses associated with owning and managing your property.

For instance, mortgage interest, property taxes, insurance premiums, and repair costs are all deductible expenses that can help reduce your taxable income. This is especially beneficial for newer property owners, as interest on a mortgage tends to represent a large portion of the monthly payment in the early years of ownership. What's even better is that depreciation, a tax benefit available to all real estate owners, can also reduce your taxable income. Depreciation allows you to deduct the loss in value of the property over time, helping to offset rental income and decrease the overall tax burden.

Furthermore, property owners can often qualify for certain tax credits, such as the Low-Income Housing Tax Credit (LIHTC), if they invest in properties that cater to affordable housing. These credits can further reduce tax liabilities, providing an incentive for investors to take on projects that may otherwise be less profitable. The tax implications of real estate investment can be complex, but with careful planning and strategy, the right deductions and credits can help make your investment a tax-efficient venture.

Deductions and Credits Every Investor Should Know

As a property investor, understanding the various tax deductions and credits available to you is critical in minimizing your tax liability. Perhaps one of the most valuable deductions is mortgage interest. In the early stages of your loan, a significant portion of your monthly payments will be allocated to interest, which can be written off. This deduction helps offset the rental income you earn, making your property more financially viable in the long run.

Beyond mortgage interest, you can deduct a wide array of expenses tied to property management. Costs like property management fees, utilities paid by the landlord, advertising expenses for filling vacancies, legal fees, and even the cost of hiring a tax professional are deductible. These expenses, which are part of the day-to-day operations of your rental property, can significantly reduce the amount of income you're taxed on, thus improving your cash flow.

Another important tax break is the depreciation of the property itself. As mentioned earlier, depreciation is a non-cash deduction that allows you to write off a portion of the property's value over its useful life. For residential properties, the IRS allows depreciation over 27.5 years, while commercial properties are depreciated over 39 years. While your property might be appreciating in value, depreciation provides you with a way to reduce your taxable income and keep more of the profits from your rental activity.

Real estate investors should also be aware of credits such as the Energy Efficiency Tax Credit, which can apply if you make improvements to the property that increase its energy efficiency. Installing solar panels, upgrading insulation, or replacing inefficient heating and cooling systems may make you eligible for these credits. These credits directly reduce the amount of tax you owe and are an excellent way to make improvements to your property while simultaneously reducing your tax liability.

Long-Term Tax Strategies for Property Investors

Long-term tax planning is essential for maximizing the profitability of your real estate investments. One of the most effective ways to reduce your tax exposure is by taking advantage of tax-deferral strategies like the 1031 exchange. This allows you to defer paying capital gains taxes when you sell a property, as long as you reinvest the proceeds into a similar investment property. A 1031 exchange can help you grow your portfolio by rolling over profits from one property to the next, all while avoiding the immediate tax hit that comes from a sale.

Another long-term strategy to consider is capital gains tax management. When you sell an investment property that you've held for over a year, your profits are generally taxed at a lower long-term capital gains rate. However, if you sell within a year, the profits are taxed as ordinary income, which can significantly reduce the amount you keep. If you are planning to sell a property, it's important to understand the timing and tax implications of that sale.

Additionally, structuring your investments properly can offer substantial tax benefits. Consider forming a limited liability company (LLC) or a real estate holding company. An LLC offers protection from personal liability while providing a more flexible tax structure, allowing you to deduct business expenses more easily. It also makes it simpler to bring on partners or investors in future deals.

Finally, consulting with a tax professional is paramount. Real estate taxation is highly nuanced, and staying on top of changing laws, regulations, and opportunities is essential. A tax professional with experience in real estate can help you navigate the complexities, find deductions or credits you might have missed, and ensure that you're making the most of your real estate investments from a tax perspective.

Real estate investing is not just about acquiring properties and collecting rents—it's also about strategically minimizing your tax liabilities. By leveraging deductions, credits, and tax-deferral strategies, you can maximize your return on investment and ensure that your real estate portfolio remains profitable over the long haul.

Chapter 10: Common Pitfalls to Avoid

"Success is the sum of small efforts, repeated day in and day out." — Robert Collier

In the world of real estate investing, even the most seasoned investors make mistakes. It's almost inevitable. But while mistakes can be part of the learning process, some missteps can be costly, both financially and emotionally. To build a successful and sustainable real estate portfolio, it's essential to be aware of common pitfalls and take proactive steps to avoid them. Here are some of the most significant mistakes that can trip up investors, and how you can sidestep them.

One of the biggest mistakes many new investors make is failing to conduct thorough due diligence. While it may seem like a time-consuming task, researching a property before making an offer is crucial. Not only should you understand the property's condition and value, but you also need to have a clear understanding of the local market conditions. Without this, you risk buying into a declining neighborhood, a property with significant hidden repairs, or a location with limited rental demand. To avoid this, always conduct a comprehensive market analysis, including property condition assessments, neighborhood trends, and comparable property sales.

Another common pitfall is underestimating the importance of cash flow. Many investors focus too heavily on the potential for property appreciation, assuming they can make up for initial losses with a future sale. However, relying on appreciation alone is risky. Cash flow—the money you make from rent after expenses—provides a more stable income stream and cushions you against market downturns. Before purchasing any property, make sure you fully understand your projected cash flow by factoring in all expenses, including property management, taxes, maintenance, and insurance. If the property doesn't offer solid cash flow, reconsider the investment or negotiate a better deal.

Overleveraging is another major mistake. While using debt to finance real estate investments can be an excellent way to scale your portfolio, it's also a double-edged sword. If you take on too much debt, it can put you in a vulnerable position if property values drop, interest rates rise, or tenants stop paying rent. Ideally, you should be comfortable with your debt-to-income ratio, ensuring that even if things go wrong, you have enough financial cushion to weather the storm. Keeping your leverage at manageable levels will allow you to make more strategic decisions without feeling trapped by high levels of debt.

Another danger lies in the emotional side of investing. It's easy to fall in love with a property or a deal, but emotions can cloud your judgment. The excitement of a potential acquisition might push you to overlook significant red flags or rush into decisions without proper analysis. Always make sure you are making decisions based on facts, numbers, and solid logic rather than getting swept up in the thrill of a deal. Stick to your investment criteria and remember that there are always more opportunities out there.

Neglecting property management is another trap that many investors fall into, especially those managing multiple properties. While you might think that property management is as simple as collecting rent and performing basic maintenance, it's a far more complex task. Tenant screening, lease enforcement, regular maintenance, and handling disputes are time-consuming and require attention to detail. Neglecting these responsibilities can result in prolonged vacancies, problematic tenants, and unexpected repair costs. Decide whether property management is something you can handle or if you should hire a professional to take care of the day-to-day operations for you. Proper management is key to ensuring a smooth investment experience.

Finally, not understanding the tax implications of your real estate investments is a costly mistake that many beginners make. Real estate offers incredible tax advantages, but without a firm understanding of depreciation, tax deductions, and other strategies, you might miss out on ways to reduce your taxable income. Consulting with a tax professional who specializes in real estate is essential for making the most of your investment. Tax planning should be part of your long-term strategy, not an afterthought.

Avoiding these pitfalls doesn't guarantee success, but it significantly increases your chances of building a profitable, sustainable real estate portfolio. By conducting thorough due diligence, managing cash flow effectively, keeping your leverage in check, and staying disciplined in your investment approach, you can navigate the often treacherous waters of real estate investing with greater confidence and success. It's all about learning from others' mistakes and using that knowledge to make smarter, more informed decisions for the future.

Mistakes First-Time Investors Make

Starting out in real estate can be an exhilarating yet nerve-wracking experience. The desire to jump into the market and start earning money quickly is understandable, but many first-time investors make a series of avoidable mistakes that can derail their success. These errors, often born out of inexperience or eagerness, can have long-lasting financial consequences. One of the most common mistakes is overpaying for property. New investors often fall in love with a property, especially after a few exciting showings or an engaging pitch from a real estate agent, only to find out later that they've paid well above market value. The best way to avoid this is to thoroughly research comparable properties in the area. This research, known as comparative market analysis (CMA), will give you a clear understanding of the fair market value and prevent you from being lured by a property that's overpriced.

Another frequent mistake is underestimating expenses. First-time investors may be so focused on the potential income from a property that they overlook the true costs of ownership. These can include property taxes, insurance, repairs, property management fees, and other hidden costs. It's vital to create a detailed budget before committing to a property. You should have a clear understanding of your cash flow projections and account for potential vacancies, repairs, and maintenance. A good rule of thumb is to overestimate expenses and have a cushion in your budget for unexpected costs.

Finally, failing to do proper research is a critical error. It's easy to get caught up in the excitement of purchasing your first property, but it's essential to approach every deal with careful analysis. Beyond just the property itself, understanding the local market dynamics, future development plans, and tenant demand in the area can make the difference between a successful investment and one that drains your resources. Take the time to research, ask questions, and talk to experienced investors or real estate agents who know the local market inside and out.

How to Avoid Overpaying for Property

One of the most significant risks in real estate investing is overpaying for a property. In the heat of the moment, especially in competitive markets, it can be easy to get carried away in a bidding war or driven by emotions, ultimately paying more than you should. Overpaying for property can severely impact your returns, making it more difficult to achieve a positive cash flow or even to sell the property later at a profit.

To avoid overpaying, the first step is to research the market thoroughly. Look at similar properties in the area, noting their sale prices and how long they've been on the market. This will give you a good sense of what constitutes a fair price. Tools like Zillow, Redfin, or local MLS listings can be valuable in this regard. But numbers alone aren't enough—you need to understand the condition of the property and any potential repairs or renovations needed. Sometimes, a seemingly good deal might require significant updates that could drastically increase your costs.

Another strategy is to engage professionals to help assess the property's true value. Real estate agents, appraisers, and even contractors can provide insights into the property's condition and its long-term value. A professional appraiser can give you an unbiased, third-party opinion on whether the property is priced appropriately, ensuring you're not overextending yourself financially.

It's also important to stick to your investment criteria. Set a budget and don't exceed it just to land a deal. Overpaying often happens when investors stray from their financial goals or get emotionally attached to a specific property. Keep your financial plan in mind and avoid the temptation to make a hasty purchase based on short-term excitement.

Navigating Legal and Regulatory Challenges

The world of real estate is filled with legal complexities. New investors often underestimate the importance of understanding the legal and regulatory requirements of property ownership. Ignorance of local zoning laws, tenant rights, or building codes can lead to costly violations, fines, or legal battles. To avoid these pitfalls, you need to do your homework and consult legal experts when necessary.

One of the first legal concerns is understanding zoning laws. These laws dictate how a property can be used—whether it's zoned for residential, commercial, or mixed-use. If you purchase a property with plans to convert it to something else, you might find that local zoning laws prevent it. This can lead to frustration, financial loss, or even forced sales. Ensure you're familiar with the zoning laws of the area, and get the necessary permits before making any changes to a property.

Another crucial legal aspect is tenant rights and responsibilities. Every state has different laws governing tenant relationships, and failing to comply with these laws can lead to costly legal issues. Understand lease agreements, security deposits, and eviction laws thoroughly before renting out a property. Whether you're managing the property yourself or hiring a property manager, make sure everyone is on the same page regarding these legal responsibilities.

Finally, building codes and inspections should never be overlooked. When buying older properties, especially those that may need renovation, ensure that any work done complies with local building codes. Failing to meet these standards can result in fines or forced repairs, eating into your profits. In some cases, properties may even be condemned if they don't meet safety standards. Always hire qualified contractors and inspectors to ensure any renovations are done legally and up to code.

By doing your due diligence and seeking professional advice where needed, you can avoid common legal and regulatory pitfalls. Understanding the rules of the game will help you maintain a smooth and profitable real estate investment experience.

Conclusion: Your Path to Building Wealth

"Success in real estate starts with the decision to take action and the willingness to learn along the way."

Real estate investing isn't just about buying and selling properties; it's a journey toward creating long-term wealth. You've now walked through the fundamentals, from understanding the market to managing risks, scaling your investments, and navigating tax laws. But the most crucial lesson? Real estate, when done right, is one of the most reliable paths to financial freedom and wealth creation.

Building a successful real estate portfolio doesn't happen overnight. It takes patience, discipline, and a commitment to continual learning. The road might be challenging at times—there will be setbacks, surprises, and hard decisions—but for those who remain focused on their goals, the rewards can be substantial. Real estate is a proven method to build wealth, and it offers a unique combination of passive income, tax benefits, equity growth, and appreciation.

One of the keys to success in real estate is recognizing that consistency matters. Just like any business, the more you invest time and effort into understanding the ins and outs of the market, the more you position yourself for success. This is especially true for beginners. The challenges of managing your first few properties or scaling up your portfolio can feel overwhelming, but each step forward provides invaluable experience that will guide your future decisions.

Don't rush the process. Start small, build your knowledge, and expand strategically. For many, this means taking the time to understand local markets, finding the right properties, and learning how to manage finances and tenants effectively. Having a solid business plan and an investment strategy is crucial to avoiding mistakes that could set you back financially. Avoid the temptation to act hastily or impulsively—successful investors know that slow, consistent growth is more sustainable in the long run.

One of the most powerful strategies you'll encounter along the way is leverage. Leverage allows you to use other people's money to finance your investments, enabling you to scale your portfolio more quickly. However, using leverage comes with risks, and it's essential to approach it cautiously. Don't overstretch yourself financially; always ensure that your cash flow is strong enough to support your debts. This is where due diligence plays a key role. By carefully researching properties, financing options, and local market conditions, you ensure you're making smart, well-informed decisions that will set you up for success.

As you grow your portfolio, remember that real estate is more than just an investment—it's also a tool for wealth protection. The right properties, properly managed, can provide financial stability, diversification, and the ability to withstand market fluctuations. Additionally, understanding the tax advantages of real estate—such as depreciation and tax deductions—can help you maximize your returns while minimizing your tax liabilities.

Ultimately, success in real estate comes down to building the right habits and mindset. Stay patient, be prepared to learn from mistakes, and surround yourself with knowledgeable professionals who can help you navigate the complexities of the market. Building wealth in real estate is a marathon, not a sprint. But for those who approach it strategically and thoughtfully, the rewards are well worth the effort.

Now that you've acquired the foundational knowledge, it's time to take action. The path to wealth through real estate is open to you. Take the first step today—research, analyze, and begin with your first investment. You don't need to know everything to start; just begin with a clear focus and a willingness to learn. The opportunities are endless, and with persistence and the right approach, you can achieve your financial goals through real estate investment. Your future wealth starts now.

How to Stay Focused and Continue Growing

Staying focused on your goals and continuing to grow in real estate requires a strong sense of discipline and a clear vision of where you want to go. You may have already absorbed the key principles of investing: due diligence, budgeting, risk management, and market analysis. But one of the biggest challenges many investors face is maintaining focus as they encounter inevitable obstacles and distractions. It's easy to become discouraged after a setback, or to get sidetracked by the next "shiny" investment opportunity that promises quick returns. But real success in real estate, as in any investment, is built over time.

The first step to staying focused is setting clear, actionable goals. Whether you're buying your first property or expanding into multi-family units, break your larger goals down into manageable chunks. Each success, no matter how small, propels you forward. This can range from securing financing, finding the right property, or negotiating your first deal.

Regularly revisit your goals and adjust them as necessary. Real estate is a dynamic field, and while your long-term strategy remains the same, you may need to adjust your approach to the market. A great way to stay grounded is to create a checklist for every step of your investing journey, helping you maintain accountability. Also, focus on building a support network—mentors, industry professionals, and fellow investors who can provide guidance and keep you on track.

The key to long-term success in real estate is persistence. You will face hurdles—market fluctuations, tough negotiations, or unexpected expenses. But remember, every challenge is an opportunity to learn and improve your approach. Keep your focus on the bigger picture and understand that success in real estate is not a sprint but a marathon.

Setting Long-Term Investment Goals

One of the cornerstones of real estate investing is setting both short-term and long-term financial goals. As you venture into this world, it's easy to get caught up in the excitement of securing your first deal or expanding your portfolio quickly. However, without a clear strategy in place, it's difficult to navigate the challenges that arise along the way.

Start by outlining specific, measurable goals that are aligned with your overall vision. What do you want your real estate investments to achieve in the next one, three, or five years? Are you looking to generate passive income, build equity, or achieve capital appreciation? Define these goals and make sure you revisit them regularly to measure your progress.

Short-term goals often revolve around acquiring your first few properties, gaining hands-on experience, and mastering the basics of property management and financing. However, your long-term goals should focus on scaling your portfolio, increasing cash flow, and building wealth over time. It's important to plan for growth—by not only adding new properties but also optimizing the ones you already own. As your portfolio expands, consider diversifying into different property types or locations to mitigate risk and increase your investment potential.

Remember, achieving long-term goals requires patience and flexibility. The market might change, your goals may evolve, but having a vision for where you want to be will help you stay motivated even during difficult times. Track your milestones, celebrate your achievements, and don't be afraid to recalibrate if necessary.

The Power of Patience in Real Estate

In real estate, patience isn't just a virtue—it's a critical asset. Unlike some other investments that promise quick returns, real estate rewards those who are willing to wait and allow their properties to appreciate over time. Whether you're purchasing residential, commercial, or rental properties, the most successful investors know that real wealth is built on the long-term.

Real estate often requires investors to weather fluctuations in the market, deal with delayed returns, or hold onto a property longer than originally planned. It's easy to become discouraged when progress feels slow, but it's essential to remember that real estate is a long-term game. Markets go through cycles, but the key is to buy strategically, manage your properties efficiently, and remain patient as you allow your investments to grow.

Consider compounding returns—as your properties appreciate in value and generate income, you can reinvest that income into new investments. Over time, this creates a snowball effect, accelerating your wealth-building process. The patience you show in letting your investments mature will pay off in ways you can't always foresee in the short term. Additionally, this mindset will help you avoid rash decisions during market downturns, instead encouraging you to hold onto your investments through volatility.

Successful real estate investors also practice patience when it comes to building expertise.

You won't know everything from day one, and that's okay. The more experience you gain, the better equipped you'll be to make informed decisions. Stay committed to learning—attend seminars, read books, and talk to industry experts to keep your knowledge fresh. Over time, this will make you more confident in your choices, enabling you to scale your portfolio with a greater sense of security.

Real estate investing is a proven path to building wealth, but it's not always a quick one. Stay patient, stay consistent, and trust that the strategies you put in place today will bear fruit in the years to come. With perseverance and a long-term mindset, you're well on your way to achieving financial success and securing your future. Remember, the best investment you can make is in yourself—your education, your strategies, and your ability to adapt. Keep moving forward, and your journey in real estate will be both rewarding and transformative.

Thank You!

Thank you for taking the time to read REAL ESTATE INVESTING GUIDE FOR BEGINNERS! I hope you found valuable insights and actionable strategies that will help you on your journey to success in real estate investing. Your commitment to learning and growing as an investor is the first step toward building long-term wealth and achieving financial freedom.

I would greatly appreciate it if you could take a moment to leave a review on Amazon. Your feedback not only helps me improve but also helps others discover the valuable content in this book. Whether it's a brief comment or a detailed review, your thoughts matter and will inspire other readers on their path to success.

If you enjoyed this book, I invite you to explore my other works available on Amazon. I have more books designed to help you grow, learn, and thrive in different areas of personal finance, real estate, and wealth-building.

Check Out My Other Books:
amazon.com/author/andyelong

Thank you once again for your support! Keep pushing forward, and I look forward to hearing about your real estate success in the future.

Best regards,
Andy E. Long.

About The Author

Andy E. Long is a seasoned entrepreneur, business strategist, and author with over 15 years of experience in the eCommerce and digital marketing industries. Known for his practical, no-nonsense approach to growing businesses, Andy has helped hundreds of entrepreneurs scale their online ventures through actionable insights, innovative strategies, and a deep understanding of market trends.

With a background in both traditional business management and the ever-evolving world of online selling, Andy has developed a keen ability to bridge the gap between tried-and-true business principles and cutting-edge digital strategies. His work spans a variety of industries, but his focus on eCommerce—particularly platforms like eBay—has made him a sought-after expert for sellers looking to break through the noise and build sustainable, profitable businesses.

Andy's approach is rooted in real-world experience. He's been in the trenches, starting businesses from scratch, learning from failures, and celebrating successes. His journey has seen him go from side hustler to full-time entrepreneur, building multiple successful online businesses along the way. Throughout this journey, Andy has maintained a focus on the power of education, customer service, and adaptability in growing a business in a competitive marketplace.

In addition to his work as an author, Andy is a sought-after speaker, mentor, and consultant. He regularly shares his expertise through online courses, workshops, and webinars, where he empowers individuals to take control of their financial futures and master the art of online sales. His unique ability to simplify complex business concepts and make them accessible to all has earned him a dedicated following of readers, students, and clients.

When he's not writing, teaching, or mentoring, Andy enjoys exploring new technologies, traveling, and spending time with his family. His commitment to lifelong learning and helping others succeed has made him a trusted voice in the world of business and money management.

www.ingramcontent.com/pod-product-compliance
Lightning Source LLC
Chambersburg PA
CBHW071026240526
45469CB00006BD/2106